The Seven Secrets of Marketing.

By the same author

Etiquette in the Business Environment
SAPPI Birds of South Africa with Callfinder
Spotter's Guide to Birds of the Bushveld (South Africa)
Spotter's Guide to Birds of the Lowveld (South Africa)
Eugène N Marais: New Facts and New Insights

Books in Afrikaans

SAPPI Voëls van Suid-Afrika met Klankleser
Kitsgids tot Voëls van die Bosveld (Suid-Afrika)
Kitsgids tot Voëls van die Laeveld (Suid-Afrika)
Eugène N Marais: Nuwe Feite en Nuwe Insigte
Oom Vaaljapie vertel.... (komiese sketse)

The Seven Secrets of Marketing
that the experts do not tell you about

Herman van Niekerk

ISBN-978-1-990988-84-4

Table of Contents

Introduction

In marketing there was the 4 P's and even the 7 P's as well as a host of other innovative tools, but the number of businesses continually failing dismally prove to us the we can still not market!

We also have a myriad of books and publications, and even dedicated computer programs on marketing, but many of them contradict each other, and it becomes difficult to work through these encyclopedias and come up with the right answers for your business.

Marketing seems to be the subject that everyone regards himself as an expert on, and probably the most written on business subject in the world. And still businesses, from huge corporations to small start-ups, fail and disappear into oblivion.

Why do they fail? Because we still do not understand marketing.

And why is that? Because there are a few simple secrets to marketing that are well guarded by the successful marketers of our time to ensure their own companies' success and to keep their competitors at bay.

Now, for the first time, the **Seven Secrets of Marketing**, or the **Seven S's** are revealed in an easily digestible way for even the layman and the novice to use and to implement as a driving factor in the success of their businesses. You can now learn these valuable lessons from the experts in this concise book!

Never before has so much potent, powerful and practical marketing communication information been packaged in such a concise, innovative, and reader-friendly book.

Who should read this book.

The company director or CEO will find this guide extremely handy in understanding marketing and asking the right questions to his marketing department and advertising agency - in fact, it will give him insight and a good measure of control.

Similarly the people involved with daily marketing duties, or novices, will gain a clear understanding of marketing and its place and function in the organization. They will even receive valuable pointers to the correct way forward.

The Seven Secrets of Marketing can change all companies' marketing behavior forever and for the better. The reader must, however, keep in mind that marketing is a vast subject and encyclopedias can and have been written about it. This book in many instances, therefore, only addresses the core issues of marketing and supply the important pointers. Further reading and study will add to the reader's knowledge in particular fields of interest.

Secret 1.
You cannot force a product into the market

No matter how hard you try, or what amount of time and money you spend on research, product development or marketing, **you cannot force a product into the market.** And you cannot sell a product by hitting consumers on the head!

The reason for this is simple: A product will only find a place in the market if it **satisfies a current need** of a group of consumers.

We hear time and again of fantastic products developed by engineers or professors, such as electric wheelbarrows or electric mouse traps, and millions being spent on the manufacturing and marketing of those products. But to no avail, because, before long, the factories are closed, the jobs and millions of Dollars lost. We read and wonder about disasters of this nature such as the Ford Edsel motor car.

The market rejected the products because there was not enough need for it. **You simply cannot force a product into the market**. Not with innovation (the Edsel) discounts or price wars, or with any amount of advertising and promotion. The market, and only the market, will decide.

What then is the answer?

You must understand the market, not the product! Your entire business must be market orientated and not product orientated. You must win over a healthy and loyal client base from the market for your product by satisfying consumer needs.

What are the basic characteristics and expectations of the consumer market:

1.   **The market expects good business practices.**
2.   **The market requires products that satisfy specific needs.**
3.   **There must be a large enough number of potential customers to make a profit from.**
4.   **The potential customers must be easily reachable.**
5.   **There must be a continuous need for the product.**
6.   **The product must be unique and set apart from its competition.**

How do you determine the characteristics of the market? By proper research of the market, and not the product! Here is what to look for and incorporate into your research, also called a market analysis:

1.   The market expects good business practices

The market expects a product that satisfies its needs, professionalism and continuous and high levels of service, honest and fair treatment, acknowledgement of human dignity and consumer rights, rewards for loyalty and adherence to the law.

Let's be honest, not everybody can do this - well, at least not without training and assistance.

Evaluate yourself and determine whether you have got what it takes to be an entrepreneur and are willing to accept the challenges. Measure yourself against the following characteristics of a typical entrepreneur:

The desire to achieve success.
Willing to be involved in the daily running of the business as owner.
To be able to reinvest profit into the business for at least 12 months.
Dedication and a willingness to work long hours.
Business acumen and management skills.
A market and marketing approach.
Good people skills and human relations.
Basic computer literacy
Independent decision making and operating.
High ethical and moral values.
Perseverance and drive.
Innovation.

If you lack skills in some of these fields, either rely on training or experience to overcome the limitations or hire or involve partners or staff to bridge those gaps.

You can also use some aspects of this handy checklist when hiring personnel.

2. The market requires products that satisfy specific needs

Make a list of types of products or areas where you have experience or knowledge of, or an interest in, when starting out with your research. You must find a product that you like and can be associated with and be proud of. You will probably enter into a lifelong relationship with that product!

Look at old products that can be rejuvenated, or entirely new products. Remember: The time in history for a product must be right. There is a right evolutionary moment for each product. There are today literally millions of patents registered in the USA and elsewhere - some are so futuristic, according to experts, that they will only materialize in 400 years. The moment in time must be right for your product.

Use a **Product Positioning Matrix** to identify possible gaps in the market for products, or acceptable changes in existing products. See Annexure A for an example of this innovative planning tool.

Also remember that some people never change their habits, while others will chase after every new product - that is why you must understand the market.

Test the envisaged products in the market in a pilot study amongst consumers.

A product, just as a human being, has a limited lifespan and a specific **Product Lifecycle.** Look for products with an historically longer lifecycle, or where you can intervene in its lifecycle and extend its lifespan. See Annexure B for more information on the very important **Product Lifecycle.**

Certain products can become obsolete overnight if they are replaced by other products performing the same functions - think of cellular phones versus pagers, ball point pens versus fountain pens, nuclear power versus coal power, etc.

Study the competitors and their products, market share, activities and marketing. You will have to face some of them head on in a challenge for the minds of the consumers.

Do consumer research and surveys.

Determine the benefits of the product, not the characteristics of the product itself. Benefits are marketed, and benefits sell products. You do not market a college, you market the benefits of a quality diploma for your customer's career and future! This is the marketing **'Promise'** which runs like a golden thread through your entire marketing strategy.

Basic human needs are food, water, clothing, shelter, safety, education, health, acceptance, assertiveness, self-esteem, reproduction, recreation, beauty and status.

Determine what needs will be addressed by your envisaged product. Look at the examples contained in the table below and expand on it.

The Marketing Promise

Basic Need	Product	Marketing Promise (Benefit)
Self-esteem, education	College diploma	A better job and quality of life
Status	Luxury car, modern house	You have arrived, other people envy you
Social interaction	Soft drink	Join the party or movement to this exclusive lifestyle
Beauty	Skin care products	Look beautiful and younger, and be envied
Health	Specific diet	Good health and quality of life; low medical bills
Safety	Martial arts training, alarms systems	Live a free life without fear

Your product must be the preferred product from all available products, and the product of first choice for a group of consumers. This is the **psychological positioning** of the product in the minds of the consumers.

People only buy and respond when the specific need arise - otherwise they don't see the advertisements at all. Test yourself. You will not see one motor car advertisement until the time that you decide to start looking for a new car - then the advertisements will suddenly pop up all over, and you will probably respond to some of them. Marketing communication is, therefore, a continuous process. New persons will enter your target market while others will leave it - there are newcomers to the job, people moving around and people dying.

Research comes first, then product development.

3. There must be a large enough number of potential customers to make a profit from

The customer base can be in a neighborhood, if we're thinking of a gardening service, or worldwide if we're thinking of selling computer programs or apps. The larger the area that you can effectively control, the higher the potential income will be. Remember, however, that the size of the market is exponential to risk. The bigger or wider the market, the bigger the risk and the likelihood that something can go wrong somewhere.

Customers have your profit in their pockets - they must spend their money at your business for you to access the profit. That is the only viable means of income that you have.

The business will only survive if it satisfies the needs of a large number of clients (client base, customer base, market share, target market, target audience). The client and only the client will decide if your business will survive or not by patronizing your business when his needs are continually satisfied or avoiding it when his needs are neglected or ignored.

You can only make a little money relevant to your total income from a single customer. The little bit of profit in each customer's pocket adds up to a substantial income if you can win and continuously service a large base of satisfied customers.

For each product there is a price band according to the customer's perception of value. He will pay about $1 for a toothbrush set, or between $20 000 and $30 000 for a motor car, according to his perceived value of what he receives. He would be prepared to pay much more for a safe and status type of motor car, than for a similar car that he does not perceive as safe and elevating his social status. He would also not buy a toothbrush set for less than $1, as his perception would be that such a cheap brush would not be of a high quality and functional for the desired job.

For every product there is a point where consumer resistance will start to take effect, with a resultant drop in sales volumes.

With luxury items consumer resistance starts at a much higher level than with ordinary, daily consumables. With luxury items more profit can thus be realized, but beware; when economic hardships arrive, these products are left on the store shelves and basic commodities such as food and medicine are bought. There are specific formulas and techniques for determining a product's ideal price band.

The customer wants value for money according to his own perceptions. It is all in the mind. Customers make the buying decision on perceived value and satisfying of needs, which include good customer relations and customer care, rather than only the specific price of an individual product.

Price is not a major factor in consumer market behavior.

4.   The potential customers must be easily reachable

You must be able to reach the potential customers with your marketing, and that is done by precisely determining your target market.   Then, secondly, the potential customers must be able to reach you.

Customers must be able to reach your product quickly and easily - they need access to your outlets, aftercare, follow-up contact and even delivery.

This is described as **physical positioning** of the product in the market (also see the sections on psychological positioning in this book)

Physical positioning includes:

Accessibility -   location of business, visibility, infrastructure, available transport, parking areas, delivery, etc.

Availability - trading hours, stock levels, number of staff to assist customers, product display, availability of product information, service.

Your business can be a food market on a busy street corner with ample parking behind it, or a catalogue or internet presence from which customers can order and have the product delivered to them by mail or courier.

Whatever mode of selling you decide on according to your business plan, ensure that the customers have easy access to the product and quick and efficient delivery.

5.   There must be a continuous need for the product

Deodorant, toothpaste, facial cream, hair shampoo and most other items are all packaged in different, funny sizes. Why? That is the amount of product, according to research, that Mr. or Mrs. Average uses in 30 days - so they must come back to the store to buy some more product for the following month and keep the factories running. You must identify a product that can give you a lifetime of value by its continuous use. Your satisfied customers must return to you continuously for more of the same product.

In the table below the **Product Time Needs of Consumers** is indicated for some products. The table gives an indication of when the consumer must or will make the buying decision. You will probably have more success and security by selling products in categories 1 to 3, which are mostly the consumables.

However, a higher profit margin in categories 4 and 5 compensate for the lower turnover and risk involved in those categories (4 and 5)

Product Time Needs of Consumers		
Category 1	Bread, milk, water, transport, telephone, soft drinks, sweets	Daily
Category 2	Vegetables, meat, gardening service, refuse removal, gasoline, fast food	Once a week
Category 3	Groceries, health and beauty care products, electricity, insurance, entertainment, investment, pool care, credit, car care products	Once a month
Category 4	Holiday, Christmas or birthday gifts, house linen, some clothing	Annually
Category 5	Motor vehicle, mortgage bond, overseas holiday, jewelry, furniture, cutlery, white goods, black goods, garden plants, shoes	Occasionally

6. The product must be unique and set apart from its competition

Identify a **position** for the product in the market to set it apart from other products in a potentially lucrative market - or create characteristics for that product to make it unique, offering special or unique benefits to consumers. Your product must have a competitive advantage over other, similar products. It must be psychologically positioned in a preferred position in the minds of the consumers.

Consumers tend to view products in classes and favor the top brand in each class. Most classes will have two successful products at the top of the class, while all the other products in that class will struggle to get a foothold in the market.

A product must preferably hold **the number one position in the minds of people** for its class. Create a new class for a product by innovation and lateral thinking if necessary. Do not include a product in other classes where distinguished market leaders already operate.

A product that is in the first place in its class is seldom pushed from that prime and lucrative position:

Mercedes Benz - first in Reliable, Status Car Class
BMW - first in Fast Car Class
Volvo – first in Safe Car Class

Virtually nothing is left for other car manufacturers to hook on to! Family cars, economical cars, anti-polluting cars, new technology cars, small cars? Not much! All other cars will in positioning lag behind the three cars who are respectively first in the important classes that count for the consumer.

Have you counted how many cola soft drinks arrived and departed over time? Get the picture?

It would be nice to sell something to everyone, but men would probably not buy lipstick, woman not neckties and children not retirement funds. Wind breakers will not do well in tropical areas, nor would ice making machines in Alaska. In many areas of the world people do not wear shoes or neckties, because of religion, custom, climate or outright poverty.

The consumer out there is also not an idiot, she is probably your wife or mother!

oooooOOOooooo

Secret 2.
You can not sell to everybody

The product that you have decided on and the need of the market will determine to whom you will sell. And that is definitely not everybody.

For ease of operations, cost-effective communication and proper aftercare, it is necessary to group the clients together in what is called a target market, market segment or client base. By herding consumers together into a coral like cattle, it is easy to work with them, communicate with them and manage them, and that is exactly what is required of a business. Communicate with and serve the selected customer base effectively.

Customers can be grouped together in two ways:

General attributes (customer profile)
Physical location (geographical area)

1. Customer profile

It is important, whilst doing your initial market analysis, to also draw up a profile of what your average customer would look like. To whom should you sell? This includes customer attributes such as:

Age
Income group
Type of profession
Gender
Cultural background (language, nationality, preferences)
Lifestyle aspects (religion, sports, hobbies, past times, entertainment)

With a solid customer profile, you would more than likely know where to find them and how to interact with them! How else does the beer moguls get to talk to the beer drinkers, or the universities to future students?   They group them together in manageable groups and talk to them en masse. That is what you should also do!

2.   Geographical area

The geographical area of your operation is very important.

In marketing you must control and dominate your territory. The area must, therefore, be of a manageable size, and coincide with the presence of a large number of members of your target audience in it.

Think of your business as a game. The game has rules, one of which is the size of the playing field. When you are outside of the playing area, you are out of bounds and cannot play.

You must decide on your business' boundaries and play within it.

What is also important is to monitor the movement of your target audience through your target area   -   public and private transport routes, stations, taxi ranks, air ports, sidewalks etc. Use a largescale map and determine and plot where your customers move throughout the day and mark the areas where they frequently pass or congregate. Look and map where they **stay, work, pray and play**   -   these are your marketing **hot spots** which is an essential element in your marketing communication strategy, as will be discussed later.

You may also find it handy to divide your target market into smaller segments and to work and conquer one segment at a time. If your business is small, you may choose to work from one street block to the next until you have conquered your entire market, or you may take one business or factory after another, according to set priorities. If you are large, however, you may segment the market otherwise. The beer people have market segments or niche markets for drinkers of light beer, ordinary beer, clear beer, dark beer, stout etc.

Because you cannot sell to everybody, you need to identify the exact profile of your target market and the geographical area where you can take control, dominate and reach and communicate with your customers easily.

oooooOOOooooo

Secret 3.
Tell your customers about their benefits

Marketing your well-researched and novel product is extremely easy, once you understand that marketing is in effect only communication. Marketing, therefore, equals marketing communication **marketing = communication**). If you can communicate, you can market.

A business is a living, growing entity or body, similar than a human being. Where a human being lives in an environment where interaction between various social structures take place, the business also exists in a business environment that interacts with it in various ways. To understand marketing communication, you must understand the business environment. Graphically the business environment looks like this:

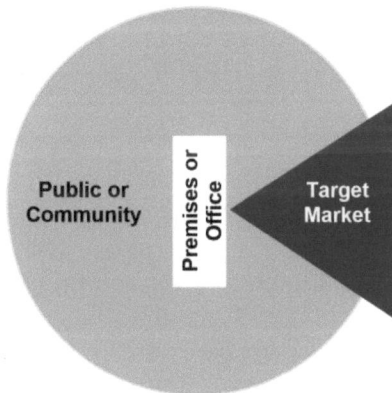

The three elements of the business environment that have an important and manageable effect on your business, are as follows:

The business, office or reception area is central to the business environment.
Secondly the target market or market segment where your customers originate from.

11

Thirdly the broad community or public in and near your area of operation.

You must, therefore, communicate with potential and existing customers in all three areas of the business's environment.

Your marketing communication tools are also threefold:

1. Service (personal contact)
2. Advertising and promotion.
3. Public relations.

Communicating effectively becomes very easy if we understand the following:

1. Service (personal contact) mostly takes place at the business premises.
2. Advertising and promotion are conducted in the target market.
3. Public relations is directed at the community or broad public in the area.

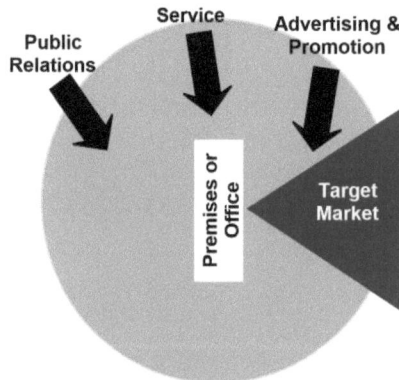

Your business must absolutely dominate in the business environment and especially in the target market to be successful.

The combined effect of proper marketing communication is as follows:

*   To enhance the business's image in the broad community in order that the community is generally positive towards the organization, and responsive to the business' advertising and promotions.

*   To get members of the target market to act on advertising and promotional campaigns and to visit the premises.
*   To win over customers and keep them with service once they have entered the premises.

The public is, therefore, systematically and purposefully drawn to the organization by effective marketing communication and convinced to become and to remain loyal customers.

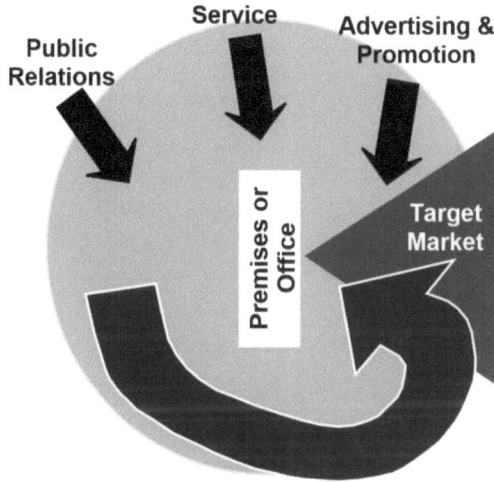

A steady flow of customers to your business is created by effective marketing communication. Remember to communicate correctly to the sector or part of the business environment you are dealing with. To repeat and emphasize:

At the business: **Service and Personal contact.**
In the target market: **Advertising and promotion.**
Amongst the public and the broad community: **Public relations.**

Each of these three modes of communication is dealt with separately in the following pages.

1. Service

Service is the major marketing communication tool used on the premises.

Service entails person to person contact (where advertising and promotion and public relations usually communicate with consumers via   medium such as a radio,

newspaper, pamphlet etc.) Service is also free. It does not cost a dime. The only thing that it can cost you, is planning, proper training, motivation and attitude.

Because good service is free, there is no excuse for bad service. Service must be excellent, in fact not just taking care of the customer's needs, but also delighting him, forcing him to come back for more! To understand service (and the other two marketing communication tools) you first need to understand the basics of communication.

Communication has the following characteristics or peculiarities, which must be considered when planning, creating or distributing communication, and especially marketing communication:

Communication does not take place by itself - it must be generated and managed. The normal trend is to communicate as little as possible, which is wrong. Communication must be properly planned. An effort must be made to communicate more, rather than less. When planning communication the 4 phases listed in the table below must be considered.

Phases of Communication

The sender	Who is he, what is his message, what is his promise to consumers, what are the benefits for consumers, who is his audience going to be.
The message	The marketing promise in simple but effective language or form. Will the receiver understand the message?
The medium	What medium will carry the message - pamphlet, newspaper, radio etc. What are their strong points and weaknesses. What are the rules for communicating through those media. Will the receiver receive the message?
The receiver	Who is he, will he be reached, will he interpret the message correctly, what must we say to spur him into action.

Back to the basics of service:

It is hard to find a definition for service. A customer will frequently say that he likes buying at Wal-Mart or Sears Roebuck but asked why, he cannot tell you.

A possible definition of service is as follows:

Service is the speed and professionalism of the businesses' actions and efforts to optimally satisfy customer needs, resulting in a congenial interpersonal relationship between the business and its customers and continued patronage.

The essence of this definition is **speed and professionalism.**

Remember also what was said earlier: In modern times people make the buying decision more on their experience related to service, than on price. Good service is, therefore, extremely important for the business' well-being.

What then, is service?

Service is the combined action of all personnel together to delight the customer. If one person in this chain of actions does not act responsibly or professionally, the chain is broken and the transaction at risk.

Personnel must, be trained and motivated to understand and practice the service concept in business. And awarded with certificates of merit and otherwise for achievements in this field (see later)

Service is also people knowledge. Personnel must really study people and know how to respond to the different types of people. Some people will always smile, while others will always be grumpy. Some will always be in a hurry, while others will have to be guided to the buying decision, some will show immediate signs of buyer's remorse and will blame it on the business, some will never be satisfied, etc.

What would the ordinary customer expect form a business:

* A friendly greeting.
* An offer for assistance and product information.
* A quality product, reasonably priced.
* Available stock.
* Warranties / guarantees.
* Aftercare.
* Packaging and delivery.
* Appreciation.
* Rectifying of mistakes.
* A general welcome feeling.
* Continuous information on the business and products.

A business must preferably have a written service manual, where everything that is expected of personnel in this regard, as well as rules and guidelines are included.

Some important guidelines for aspects to be included in the service manual, are the following:

1.1 Office hours:

Punctuality - service must be available during publicized trading hours. Personnel must be punctual.

1.2 Appearance:

The business must always appear neat and clean.

The customer must associate with items in the business such as lay-out, plants, paintings, etc. Beware of religious or political emblems or icons - they may scare customers away.

Keep noise levels in the business low - especially if you play music on the premises.

Clean the business after hours and pack shelves after hours if possible.

Have a regard for customer safety - wet floors, electrical installations, security.

1.3 Courtesy:

A customer that enters a business must be greeted immediately and his presence acknowledged, even if you cannot service him immediately.

Every customer is greeted with a smile and a welcome greeting.

One never talks down to or quarrel with a customer. Use neat but simple language, evading difficult and technical jargon.

Be tactful, use diplomacy and be consistent.

Personnel should be able to identify different types of customers with ease: Difficult, eccentric, grumpy, arrogant, normal, indecisive, buyer's remorse, never satisfied, unreasonable, wants company to change policy just for him, hunt for bargains, etc.

1.4 Product offering:

Quality, quantity.
Information.
Range.
Display.
After care (delivery, warranties and service)

1.5 Problem solving:

Problems are solved immediately and refunds or apologies offered, or rectifying steps taken.

A complaints and compliments book can be at the disposal of customers and they should be encouraged to make use of it.

A procedure for handling complaints must be determined - what must the customer do and who in the business takes responsibility. Where can he complain if he does not get satisfaction from the business.

1.6 Training and education:

Train personnel in what is required of them regarding service, people skills, product knowledge, negotiation skills, conflict handling, problem solving, organizational skills, etiquette and company policy and vision.

Educate customers regarding company policy, product knowledge, new product information and complaints and compliments procedures.

1.7 Customer affiliation program:

Customers like to support a winner.   Customers also like to be acknowledged and obtain benefits for patronizing a business and for goals or achievements reached, which will ensure their loyalty.

Implement affiliation programs whereby loyal customers can obtain benefits such as free entry into competitions, specific discounts, free services such as delivery, etc. See Section 4 below for more information on this.

A satisfied customer will patronize the business continuously. He will also refer his friends and family to your business. It is easier and cheaper to continuously sell to satisfied customers, than to market aggressively for new customers every month.

70% of clients reverting to other businesses give service, or rather a lack of proper service, as the reason why they did not remain loyal to that business in the first place. It is a sin to lose a satisfied customer with shoddy service!

A client that is not satisfied will on average tell 11 other people of his negative experience about you, killing your customer base. A satisfied client will only tell 3 people about your good service.

An increase of only 1% in the service levels of your business can increase turnover with as much as 10%.

Let us list some service sins:

Not prepared.
Not willing to listen and understand the customer's needs.
Talking too much.
No respect for the client.
Not positive towards the business and not motivated.
Inadequate product knowledge.
Not able to answer customers' questions.
Pre-occupied by private matters
Receiving visitors at work
Not communicating well.
Unfriendly.
Slow and listless.

Practical experience

It may be worth your while to enlist people from the street, or potential customers, at the cost of a gift to engage with personnel in a mock transaction to expedite the personnel's experience levels in this manner and to ensure that personnel have the knowledge and the ability to handle real customers

---

The service levels of your business must be measured from time to time in consumer surveys. Ask the customers directly what they think about your Three P's - **Product, Personnel** and entire consumer **Package**. Ask questions about the aspects mentioned above.

Also ask the customers for suggestions on what they would like to see in the business. This will make them feel involved, acknowledged and respected, and supply you with guidelines for the future.

After your customer surveys: Adapt or die!

An important part of service in the business is the way you handle and deal with customers - albeit personally, by letter, telephone, sms, e-mail, mobile phone or fax. In these instances specific customer etiquette applies.

Service is the most important aspect of keeping and maintaining customers. It is, therefore, planned and managed on management level. Good service is compulsory and non-negotiable.

2.   Advertising and promotion

Your second important marketing communication tool is Advertising and Promotion. Your business has probably already been established and personnel trained in providing service that delight the customers.

You have probably also identified your target market. Now you must start to communicate with them.

Communicating with your target market is the most expensive part of your three-tier marketing communication strategy. That is because you are not in a position to talk to all the potential customers personally, but you must rely on intermediate tools such as newspapers, the radio, pamphlets, brochures, video's, social media etc. to communicate with them.

You must also dominate in your target market, which means a high level of presence and a large amount of (costly) promotional (or publicity) material. The reasons why you must dominate in your chosen target market or playing field are twofold:

1:   You must continuously inform the consumers about your product and benefits and position your product in their minds as the first or best in its class, so that they can respond when the need for the product arises by buying your product.

2:   You must dominate to illustrate to any competitors envisaging intruding on your target area that you are active and effective, thus keeping them at bay.

How do you dominate in your target market? With:

Logo.
Outdoor advertising.
Other advertising and promotional material (effective distribution)
Infiltration.

2.1 Logo

The business must have a distinct name, logo and colors, and if appropriate also a slogan and a jingle, that is used to identify it with and set it apart from its competitors. Just think of the prominent McDonalds M in this regard. This is known as the corporate image and is a major contributing factor to sales and customer loyalty.

The corporate image items are usually created by experts in their respective fields after a substantial amount of research and is legally protected as trade or registered marks and/or copyrighted.

The elements of the corporate image are the crown jewels of the business. Its use is precisely described in a corporate manual, and strictly enforced. The logo is correctly displayed on all material of the business. It is always taking prominence over any other logos. It is never changed. Nothing is ever printed over it. No other person or institution except your business may use it in any way without your written permission.

See the information on logo's in the Hints section of the book.

2.2 Outdoor advertising

Outdoor advertising is, in fact, just what it says. It is advertising material erected outside of the business premises and include billboards, posters, signs, flags, banners, vehicles with livery on, stickers, bumper stickers, dustbins, gazebo's, permanent stands, painted walls or fences etc. People wearing placards and moving along streets are also regarded as outdoor advertising! There are no new outdoor advertising wonders - it is still all the same old stuff, and it still works wonders!

Outdoor advertising is normally expensive to create and/or erect, but once in place it is relatively cost-effective as you would only have low monthly rental fees to pay for the space and a minimum of maintenance. However, in many instances free space for advertisements can be negotiated, sometimes in return for favors such as mowing a lawn regularly or maintaining a fence around a property.

Outdoor advertising must be erected where the members of your target market can see it regularly. Earlier we described how you have to identify the **'Hot Spots'** in your target market - those areas where potential customers pass frequently.

Erect outdoor advertising at your **hot spots** and make sure that potential customers do not move around in the target area for longer than 10 minutes without seeing some of your outdoor advertising, even if it is just as a reminder.

Prioritize the **hot spots** and erect your outdoor advertising according to a program over time in order that you may dominate in this field in, say, 6 months or a year's time.

The business front (on street level) is part of the outdoor advertising and must be neat, attractive, colorful, recognizable and distinguishable from competitors. Use flags and moving elements to attract more attention to it.

Maintain your outdoor advertising and keep it clean, neat and tidy. The important thing of outdoor advertising is to place it at proven ***hot spots*** where the customers can see it regularly and be guided to your business by arrows, addresses, telephone numbers and reminders.

2.3 Other advertising and promotional material

Once your outdoor advertising is in place, you turn to other advertising material and promotional items to attract attention to your business.

Advertising material and promotional items have a short lifespan, compared to outdoor advertising, and is considered and used virtually daily.

These items always display your distinct business logo, your marketing promise to your potential customers and normally your list of products and prices, as well as an invitation to visit you.

Once again there is nothing new that will suddenly turn your business around: We are still using flyers, brochures, newspaper and magazine advertisements, shows, fairs and exhibits, radio and TV or Internet and social media advertisements, telephone calls

or messages or advertisements on mobile phones, in-store promotions and different types of competitions.

The important thing about this other advertising material and promotions is to distribute the material effectively amongst your target market, and only your target market. You must not shoot with a shotgun in a general direction. You must ensure that the radio, newspaper or magazine advertisement reaches your target market.

Newspapers and magazines can usually supply you with figures regarding the print order and number of readers per area, while TV and radio networks, and web page and social media hosts can supply you with similar, independently researched information.

Distribute pamphlets effectively in your target area.

Placement of advertisement

A newspaper or magazine advertisement on a righthand page is more effective than one on a left hand page, and one on the top half of a page is more effective than one on the bottom half of a page.

An important feature of these advertisements and promotions is to lure potential customers to your business premises - the must come and physically see the business and the products on display, and your personnel must have the opportunity to meet and interact with them.

Completed competition forms must, therefore, be placed in a container on the premises, and competition questions must be answered after certain information have been obtained on the premises.. Lucky draws etc. must be conducted on the premises.

The Contents of a written advertisement

A catchy heading or slogan summarizing the promise to the potential customer.
The logo and business identity.
A photograph or sketch to draw attention.
Body copy expanding on the customer promise.
Contact numbers and addresses.
An invitation to act immediately.

The Contents of a radio advertisement

You only have 30 seconds (or less) to impress the listener or potential customer:
Repeat the company name and customer promise at least three times -
beginning, middle and end.
Do not include annoying sounds with the hope of attracting attention.
Do not use alarm, telephone or a barking dog sounds – it may startle people.
If you use a jingle, use a catchy one.
Be brief and to the point.
Provide information - do not entertain.
Concentrate on the customer promise.
Tell the potential consumer what to do next.

The Contents of a Television advertisement

Visual impact is important.
The logo must appear on the screen from the beginning right through to the end,
and can, in fact, move from one position to another.
Sound must be at the normal level -   customers are irritated if they have to turn
the volume of their sets down continuously, and irritated customers do not buy.
Use a theme that potential customers will remember and associate with.
Use simple language and content.
Look for something potent.
Don't be funny - buying product is a serious business for customers.
Provide information, do not entertain.
What you want to say can really be said in 15 to 20 seconds - anything longer is
unnecessary padding to enrich people who claim that they are copywriters.

Words that attract most attention in advertisements:

Free, new, save, best, unique, service, need, money, once in a lifetime, sale,
money back offer, hurry, while stocks last, only two per customer, do not miss
this offer, only for a select few, contact us today, free gift, limited offer, only at
this low price until (date and time), you'll expect to pay much more for this.

2.4 Infiltration

Infiltration is a referral system whereby satisfied customers refer other people to your business. Such helpful customers are referred to as **'Champions.'**

Ideally such champions should be in place for you at every large employer or places where large numbers of people gather such as clubs, schools, churches and societies.

The champion is the opinion maker in that particular circle of society and used to distribute your business' information informally and orally to the rest of that institution's staff.

Champions need training about your business and products to be able to fulfill their roles successfully. They must also be proud to be associated with you.

The champion may be a member of your affiliate program and receive benefits from it. Infiltration is handled circumspectly.

Some important marketing quotes

If you believe in your business, market it.

Marketing is an investment in your business and your future.

The market (potential customers) must be taken seriously.

Marketing is the collective wisdom of the business.

Your marketing is as strong as your weakest employee.

---

3. Public relations

The last but also important marketing communication tool is your public relations program.

This program is the one that you use to communicate with the community in general in your area with the aim of creating and maintaining a good public image.

Every individual would have an opinion of your business, based on knowledge obtained from experience, publications, broadcasts or from views of other people.

It is important that this public opinion of your business is favorable, because, as was discussed earlier, this is an important step, and actually the first step, in channeling potential customers to your business.

Businesses are easily stereotyped by the public at large, and such images can harm the individual business tremendously. We frequently hear that all realtors are crooks and all financiers loan sharks. Such stereotypes can cost you your business and must be avoided or rectified by maintaining a proper public relations program.

3.1   What then is public relations?

Public relations is a purposeful and continuous, pro-active communication process by an organization whereby it aims to effect permanent changes in members of its target market's attitudes and perceptions by an honest and open appeal on people's reason.

3.2 What can public relations do for an organization?

Public relations can:

Create a climate for healthy and sustainable business.
Change attitudes and perceptions over time.
Inform the public.
Orientate the target market.
Place events in context and prevent rumors.
Relay messages quickly and effectively.
Support the service of the business and its advertising and promotion.
Inform and motivate personnel.
Appeal on people's reason.
Apologize on behalf of the business and inform public of rectifying steps.
Limit damage.

3.3 What can public relations NOT do for an organization?

Public relations CAN NOT:

Redress mistakes.
Tell lies.
Protect the business or personnel members.
Make propaganda.
Appeal on people's emotions.

Spread false rumors.
Create or promote an image that does not exist.
Attack or slander competitors.
Avoid the issue.

Public relations has two fields, namely internal and external public relations.

With an internal public relations program standards are set and personnel motivated to become part of the winning team. Once this is in place, the external public relations program is enacted.

Tools for the internal public relations program are training, letters of welcome, meetings, notice boards, information sessions, participatory management, circulars, personnel newsletter, awards, personnel promotion, team building etc.

Because we cannot individually talk to every possible customer out there, we must mostly use the mass media to communicate with them. The mass media are newspapers, magazines, radio, television and the internet, social media, public meetings, shows, exhibitions etc. where applicable. We can also communicate with the target market by way of meetings, publications such as annual reports, etc. However, the mass media are the important tools in public relations.

To use the mass media as free communication tools you need to do the following:

3.4 Identify the appropriate media

Identify the relevant media in your target market that you can possibly use as communication tools. Especially look at local media such as local radio stations, knock-and-drop neighborhood newspapers, church newsletters, school and club newsletters etc.

It may even be worth your while to start a newsletter for a club or school with your business as sponsor if you can control the advertising content and distribution to your target market.

3.5 Make friends with the journalists / reporters / editors / owners

Identify the key personnel at the different media identified, meet with them, make them your friends and come to some sort of mutually beneficial arrangement with them regarding time or space for news and assistance or sponsorships from your business. The average journalist will much more readily accept news given to him on a platter, than going out there on his own to hunt for news.

3.6 Create and supply NEWS to them

The media thrives on NEWS and only NEWS! Create news about your business and supply it to your friends at the media for publication: Annual report, growth figures, competition details and dates, prize winners, product promotions, new product lines, business extensions, staff promotions, etc.

You may even become an expert and spokesperson for the industry you are in if you obtain and update the relevant knowledge and supply it as industry information and statistics to the media on an ongoing basis. You will, in fact, later be quoted as an expert in your field. And consumers would like to be acquainted to you.

But the purpose of all this is to generate favorable comment from the public and to create a good public image for your business.

Some other components of an external public relations program may be:

Annual report.
Public meetings (AGM)
Selective sponsorships.
Press releases.
Press conferences.
Media tours.
Open days.
Image building advertisements (paid)
Personal letters.
Greeting and other cards.
Selective gifts of promotional articles.
Membership of and active participation in trade or business associations.
Aid and assistance to the poor and the needy.
Donations to disaster funds.
Contributions to education or wildlife protection and conservation.
Bursaries, always related to your core business or product!
Free service by staff members at hospitals, animal welfare shelters etc.
Projects to clean up the streets and the area around your town, city or business district.
Transport for the elderly to and from clinics, hospitals, shopping centres etc.

Beware of donations, assistance and support to political parties, religious groups, confrontational organizations and newly found organizations who not yet have a good track record. Your reputation could be at risk.

Some guidelines on sponsorships:

A sponsorship is basically a form of advertising and you need to get your money's worth from it. Evaluate what it is worth to you.

Ensure that such a sponsorship can in some positive way be connected directly to your business or sector - for example mining and the environment, fishing and marine conservation, medicine and bursaries for medical students.

Be wary of sponsorships for political parties, religious entities and cultural activities limited to specific cultures, classes or groups.

Determine what your responsibilities are in terms of the sponsorship, and what the receiver's reciprocal responsibilities are. Write this down in a sponsorship agreement.

Pay over amounts of the sponsorships after certain targets have been met by the receiver, and not the entire amount up front.

Manage the sponsorship daily, just as you would manage any other important business function.

Ensure that personnel understand the reasons for the sponsorship and associate with the cause.

Ensure that positive information about the sponsorship is extensively used in your public relations program.

In your marketing communication to your customers and potential customers make sure that you include the AIDA-principle. All individual marketing communication items or projects as well as the combined plan and strategy must embrace the AIDA-principle and involve the customer as follows:

A = Attract **Attention**

I = Create **Interest**

D = Create **Desire**

A = Spur on to **Action**

Also ensure that the following communication **SINS** do not creep in amongst personnel in your marketing communication program:

Not listening.
Not identifying the customer's request / need.
Talking too much.
Not loyal to own product and brand.
Not able to supply product knowledge.
Using difficult language and words.
Using highly technical language and descriptions.
Talking about non-related matters.
Referring customers to opposition.
Wasting time.
Be a know-all.
Prejudice.
Rudeness.
Too hurried.
A superior attitude.

ooooo OOO ooooo

Secret 4.
Get your satisfied customers to talk to one another

Earlier in this guide the importance of a definite target market and a healthy, increasing client base were discussed.

The service concept was described as the optimal tool for creating customer delight, and for realizing continuous business and profit from the same client. You must receive life-long support and benefits from customers. The so-called lifetime value.

This is achieved by effective marketing communication to the members of your target market (see previous section)

However, this is not where it ends, and one important aspect remains to be addressed: **You must get your satisfied customers to talk to one another!**

Why?

By getting customers to talk to one another you:

Expand your sales force multifold.
Spread the message in a receptive environment.
Get marketing communication for free.
Make optimal use of social media.
Your marketing works for 24 hours a day across any type of border.
You are at the forefront of the new, future dimension in marketing.

The traditional marketing communication is sometimes negatively referred to as **'Interruption Marketing'** because you as the advertiser would interrupt a potential customer's private time and space with you marketing communication.

Graphically it can be illustrated as follows:

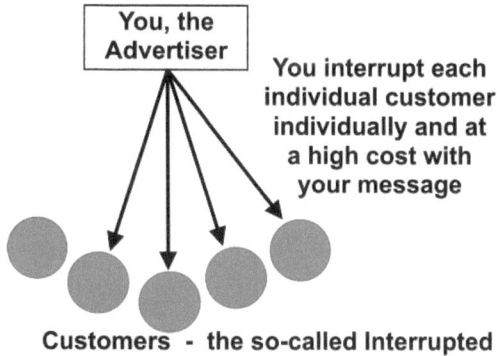

You interrupt each individual customer individually and at a high cost with your message

Customers - the so-called Interrupted

I personally do not think the term interruption marketing with its negative connotations describes the process correctly.

Traditional marketing is not wrong or negative marketing at all, and vast empires have been built on marketing communication of this nature. It must therefore be continued, but perhaps in a more refined way. The important concept of getting customers to talk to one another and for them to market on your behalf must be added to that.

What you would like to happen, is this:

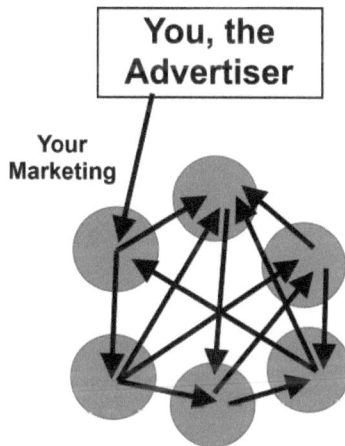

Let's be honest - this was always done, but perhaps on a limited scale. There is nothing new to referrals and word-of-mouth marketing. But it is becoming more and more important as a communication tool to sell product with.

I would like to introduce two new terms for the two levels of marketing under discussion, as follows:

Primary Marketing - where you directly use one or more of the three marketing communication tools - service, advertising and promotion or public relations.

Secondary Marketing - where you enlist satisfied customers to market on your behalf.

Seth Godin calls this **Secondary Marketing 'he ideavirus.'** His book, **'Unleashing the Ideavirus'** from which reference work some information has been obtained for this section of my book, is acknowledged and recommended for further reading.

We must understand the importance of **Secondary Marketing** and one way to do this is to take note of some of the research findings or comments of other respected marketers regarding the present position of **Primary Marketing** as listed in the Table below.

After everything has been said, it is still a fact that you cannot market to a consumer who is not receptive and intent on listening. Note the difference between hear and listen. Hearing is receiving sounds, but listening is interpreting them!

You must therefore create a healthy balance between proven **Primary Marketing** whilst also establishing an effective **Secondary Marketing** network. In fact, start-up businesses may find it more cost effective to also place the emphasis on **Secondary Marketing** at the outset.

Modern day comments on Primary Marketing.

More and more products are daily screaming for attention to survive.

Unanticipated, impersonal, irrelevant advertisements flood the consumer environment in a vain hope of selling product.

Interruption marketing worked because consumers needed some products and there was no other reliable source of information.

Consumers are overawed by the flood of advertisements and escape them by ignoring them or running to the loo.

Advertisements are appearing everywhere and consumers cannot distinguish or select between the daily clutter anymore.

Customers do not respond to unwanted marketing messages anymore.

You cannot market to consumers by annoying them.

Consumers have too much power and too little time to respond to invasive advertising.

There is an uncontrolled, international consumer movement developing that actively resists invasive marketing.

Advertisements are appearing in unheard of places such as hotel elevators, toilets and public telephone booths in a desperate effort to get some sort of message through to consumers.

Advertisements are generally becoming more expensive and less effective.

In **Secondary Marketing** customers talk and listen to each other, likeable to testimonials, voluntarily and unhindered. The situation is, therefore, conducive to proper communication between the sender and the receiver of the marketing message or "promise" to the consumer. This is the major benefit of **Secondary Marketing** over **Primary Marketing**.

4.1 How to do Secondary Marketing

Create customer networks, get customers to talk to one another about your product and stand back. These customers are your 'champions' in marketing and talk to one another. Then bestow benefits on the champions in your customer networks.

This can be likened to some sort of affiliate program, and possibilities are endless.

4.2 How to create a network

Identify existing satisfied (delighted) clients.
Ensure that they are opinion makers in their respective areas (place of work, church, school, club. society etc.)
Ensure that they are likeable and can communicate well.
Recruit them as champions.
Train them regarding the company, business and products in general.
Inspire them.
Let them loose in the market.
Keep them up to date and informed.
Keep them happy (see next paragraph)

4.3 How to keep your champions happy

Earlier we described the satisfying of certain basic needs as a universal human attribute. Some of these needs are solely related to vanity - status, self-esteem, acknowledgement, in fashion, with it!

If you can satisfy a customer's needs in these fields of vanity by an affiliation program, he will become and remain a loyal champion.

You must, therefore, create an atmosphere or lifestyle, virtually as members of an exclusive club, for your champions.

In fact, in this 'club' there should be different categories of champions, each receiving different benefits. New customers and junior members must do everything in their power to advance to the higher level of the club and receive the increased benefits. And part of the criteria is, of course, sales volumes!

Your hierarchy could look like this:

Level E   -   New customers.
Level D   -   Customers of 1 year standing and purchases of $x.
Level C   -   Champion Class C – determine own criteria.
Level B   -   Champion Class B – determine own criteria.
Level A   -   Champion Class A – determine own criteria.

Your permanent benefits could include the following:

Discounts on purchases (except for level E)
Gift vouchers (which is spent in your business)
Free holiday weekends, vacations or trips.

Free movie tickets.
Free training seminars.
Advance viewing of new products.
Regular get together events - business functions / meetings / social events. Christmas parties and gifts for their children

Give them status, a sense of purpose and a sense of belonging.
Raise their standard of living.

(NS: Many of the benefits need not be funded from your own pocket - you would surely have some suppliers who would like to come to the party with free product or funds – it is ultimately also in their best interest)

You must create a unique concept where consumers would aspire and like to belong to. You must give them an opportunity in life to move ahead. They must see you as part of their future. Then the consumers will start talking to each other about the concept, thus marketing you, your business and your product.

It is up to you to create this unique concept, to enroll the right people as champions and to instill the concept into the market. And everybody must long for the concept and want to participate because:

It is the new fashion and norm.
It is got hype and is a wow-idea.
It is exciting.
It is innovative, fresh and modern.
It is newsworthy and consumers talk about it.
It is providing real benefits for champions.
It is leading the market.

It is up to you, and only you, to get a team of satisfied customers to voluntarily talk to one another and sit back and reap the benefits.

ooooooOOOooooo

Secret 5.
Motivate the people working for you

It is common knowledge that motivated and positive personnel contribute in various ways to the prosperity of the business, including:

Maintaining healthy client relations.
Increasing sales.
Creating an esprit de cor or benevolent company culture or spirit.
Creating a happy working environment.
Influencing other personnel member's behavior positively.
Increasing productivity.

Apart from hiring the right person with the necessary people skills and development potential, you, and only you, must ensure that personnel are motivated. Here are **Thirteen Tools** that you may enlist in this regard:

* Remunerate properly and for performance. Think of bonus systems for achievement and remember personnel's needs such as medical aid and pension funds. Benchmark salaries with industry standards.

* Acknowledge achievements by accolades, certificates and public presentations, and use in your public relations program.

* Introduce reasonable performance targets or goals and help personnel to achieve them. Your best people should work with your customers, and if they get paid more than the boss, it is only an indication of their motivation and contribution to the well-being of the company! It is not wrong. It is not a sin.

* Talk to personnel regularly and frankly about their work and performance. Discuss ways to overcome obstacles or problems encountered. Give reasons for decisions.
* Allow personnel and pay for membership of trade associations or chambers that will further their careers and your business and where they can promote company matters.

* Identify leaders and create training, development and promotion opportunities.

* Create social opportunities where personnel can socialize and learn from and talk to one another such as business lunches, in house seminars and social evenings.

* Allow personnel unrestricted membership of trade unions and establish a responsible relationship with such unions.

* Inspire a culture of life-long learning and assist with time or money to enable personnel to advance their training.

* Establish a complaints and grievances procedure.

* Involve personnel in participatory management. Let them feel that they belong and that their contributions and input are welcome, appreciated and valued.

* Keep personnel informed about company matters - regularly present them with sales figures, future outlook, new developments, product information, forthcoming changes, company expectations, company policy.

* Remember that personnel have a life outside of the business as well. Allow and assist personnel within reason to develop their family and social lives outside of the office. Respect their private time.

If you are unable to motivate your personnel on a continuous basis, you may just as well kiss your business goodbye!

oooooOOOooooo

Secret 6.
You must adapt or die

In a changing world there is one universal law: Adapt or die. Because change will inevitably occur, either self-inflicted or because of uncontrollable outside factors.

In business you have to adapt, and you have to adapt regularly, sometimes even overnight, to survive!. That is the law! That is the fact!. A mere thirty years ago mobile phones and the internet and social media were new words to many people. Today they are major contributors to every business' success. We had to adapt to that.

New laws on the statute books also force us to adapt. The introduction of new products to the market by our competitors, or changes in consumer behavior, also requires of us to look at our business in a new way, and to make changes.

What do you adapt to, and how do you adapt? You cannot change anything in your business just for the sake of change or to follow trends or your competitors. There must be a sound reason for any change to your business. If not, unnecessary changes can harm your business, as indicated in the table below:

The Effect of Uncontrolled Changes in the Business

Changes may make your customers uncomfortable.
Changes my make personnel anxious, especially about their careers and future.
Changes may worry your suppliers.
Changes may make your bankers and financiers ask uncomfortable questions.
Changes may cost a lot of money.

Your basis for change is, once again, research. Apart from the market research before initiating your business, you will also embark on a process of continuous research during the lifespan of your business regarding your market, product and business.

You will look at sales figures and relevant company information monthly. However, from time to time you would like to have additional knowledge to base your business management decisions on, such as:

What does the market say?
What product developments are foreseen?
What does the competition do?
How do the personnel feel?

Dedicated companies specializing in research can be contracted to do this type of research. However, a lot can also be done by utilizing own resources to develop questionnaires and interpret the data with the aid of, for instance, students.

There are also other means of obtaining information as listed below.

How to obtain strategic business information

Surveys by established research institutions amongst your target audiences.
Enlisting the services of qualified consultants.
Own questionnaires and surveys amongst target audiences.
Research from publications (libraries / internet / trade magazines)
Dedicated research on specific topics by universities or relevant institutions (or post graduate students)
Buying of specialist annual consumer surveys.
Studying of competitors' annual reports, press releases etc.
Studying of competitors' marketing communication.
Internet surveys

Here is the type of questions that you need to ask in a customer survey:

6.1 What does the market say

What needs do they have related to your product?
Are they satisfied with the quality / range of your product(s)?
Are they happy with the appearance and lay-out of your business?

Are they happy with your personnel and their product knowledge?
Are they happy with your service?
Are they happy with your business hours?
Are they happy with your aftercare service?
What do they think about stock levels/variety?
What do they think about delivery?
What is your market share?
What do they think of competitors and their products?
Do they have any suggestions for improvement?

6.2 What product developments are foreseen

(A suggested study at universities, manufacturers, suppliers, importers, patent offices, etc.)

Are there any new developments regarding your range of products?
Will some of your products become obsolete and how will it affect the business?
Would the replacement products be a viable alternative?
What funding in stock levels and training would be required for new products?
Have the new products been tested amongst consumers and what was the reaction?
Would parts for maintenance of the old products remain available?
When and how will the new products be introduced?
What are the advantages for the consumer?
What will the effect on product price be for the consumer?
Can my staff be retrained to handle a new product range?

6.3 What the competition does

(Study competitor's available documentation and monitor their conduct)

What is their market share?
What is their product promise?
What is the essence of their marketing communication strategy?
How much funding do they have available for marketing?
What is their long-term vision?
How do they handle competitors?
Do they plan expansion? (Steve Job once announced that Apple is going to re-invent the cellular phone)
What are the points that you are stronger than them, and can attack them on?

6.4 How do the personnel feel

(An in-house confidential survey)

How do the personnel feel about:

Salaries.
Staff benefits.
Working conditions.
Future career with company.
The product.
The business ethos.
The company and its future.
Possible changes in products of the company
Changes expected from staff after required company adjustments/re-inventions.
Are there any suggestions for change or improvement?

Surveys -   important notes

Limit the number of questions to the essential.

Use simple, easily understandable language.

Test questions beforehand to ensure relevancy and understandability.

Let customers fill out a monkey-puzzle on a scale from 1 to 5 for each question.

Do not waste customers' valuable time.

Let participants feel that they make a valuable contribution.

Acknowledge their input.

Hand them a small gift.

Inform them of the outcome of the survey.

---

ooooooOOOooooo

Secret 7.
You must work according to a plan

Earlier in this publication we likened the business to a game that is played on a specific field. The truth is, however, that business is anything but a game.

* Business is you and your personnel's only source of an income and earning a living.
* Business is a continuous war between competitors - dog eats dog.
* Business is a struggle for the hearts and minds (and pockets) of consumers.
* Business is satisfying consumer needs to the utmost.
* Business is your future.
* Business is your quality of lifestyle.
* Business is your time and quality of retirement

Business is serious stuff!

Business is, therefore, not done on the spur of the moment, as a pastime or haphazardly. Business is planned and managed professionally on management level by professional people.

Various strategies, policies and plans must, therefore, be in place in the business. A vision and mission for future growth, a personnel policy, a training policy, a service manual, a corporate manual etc.

The most important planning document is, however, your marketing communication plan. This plan, with its tentacles reaching to virtually every other section of your business, is the one, crucial element in the success of your business.

The marketing communication plan is:

* Based on research.
* Involves all personnel members.
* Establish reporting lines.
* Sets targets.
* Is management by objectives.
* Allows for measurement and control.
* Allows for adaptation.

Here are the 25 important elements of your marketing communication program:

1. Involve the owner (or shareholders) in the business daily and obtain his written commitment, financial and otherwise, to the business.

2. Appoint or designate a senior person in writing with the responsibility of planning and executing marketing communication.

3. Involve all personnel in the marketing communication planning and execution.

4. All personnel is orientated and trained in marketing communication.

5. Introduce personnel motivational systems and programs.

6. The market is analyzed to determine its needs and potential.

7. The exact target market and operational area of the business is determined.

8. Develop or refine the product and product offering according to market needs.

9. Determine the business' vision or long term goal.

10. Determine the business' mission or strategy to reach its long term goal.

11. Draw the break-even graph for the business to determine growth targets.

12. Incorporate marketing communication as a core function in all personnel's duty sheets.

13. Work according to and provide funding for marketing communication in a proper marketing budget.

14. Maintain the corporate identity Immaculately.

15. Dominate continuously in your target market.

16. Establish your affiliation program for champions and infiltrate areas where large numbers of consumers congregate.

17. Maintain the service concept and delight the customers.

18. Implement a sound public relations program.

19. Accept and practice social responsibility.

20. Study, monitor and counter competitors.

21. Co-ordinate marketing communication in the business.

22. Introduce work schedules.

23. Introduce management by objectives.

24. Measure results and trends.

25. Adapt.

When you have researched and implemented the 25-steps above, you would have, in fact, implemented a comprehensive marketing communication plan in your business.

In Annexure C a Pro Forma Marketing Communication Plan is included as a guideline with additional information to create and implement one for the business. Remember that this plan is not a monthly or annual once-off - the marketing communication plan is a living document, used, changed and adapted continuously.

oooooOOOooooo

I trust that The Seven Secrets of Marketing not only gave the reader valuable insight into the all important marketing facet of an organization, but that it also will contribute substantially to the reader and his company's well-being and lasting financial success.

Herman van Niekerk

Annexure A
The Product Positioning Matrix

New Product development is the lifeblood of an organization. This has, therefore, become a specialist field in marketing, with many consulting companies specializing in it. Computer programs have even been developed to assist with new product identification and development. There are also ways and means of shortening product development time.

One of the most effective tools to analyze a market with and to identify possible new products, or changes to products, is a **Product Positioning Matrix (PPM)**

The matrix is a diagram consisting of four squares and scaled on both axes from 1 to 10. The blank matrix looks like this:

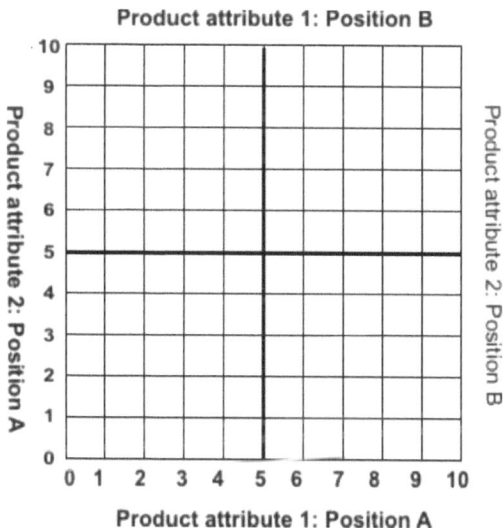

Product attribute 1: Position B

Product attribute 2: Position A

Product attribute 2: Position B

Product attribute 1: Position A

Sets of two attributes of existing products In the market are researched and plotted on the matrix. For each product there would, therefore, eventually be a number of matrixes. The attributes are each scaled on a scale of one to ten: If price would be an attribute, the scale would start from cheap and end at expensive. If color would be an attribute the scale would start at white and end at colored or colorful. If taste would be an attribute the scale can start at sour and end at sweet. The number of attributes that can be chosen is limitless.

Various similar products in the market are then studied and compared and the information plotted on each matrix. After this has been done, gaps in the market can be seen easily, and products to fill that gap investigated.

The following example shows what a **PPM** can tell you. In this instance 2 characteristics of seven brands of toothpaste have been researched:

Product attribute: Texture coarse

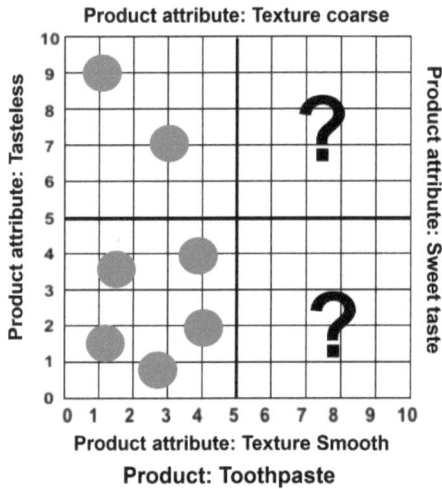

Product attribute: Tasteless

Product attribute: Sweet taste

Product attribute: Texture Smooth

Product: Toothpaste

No present product fills the marketplace of the two squares on the right side of the diagram. The question marks, therefore, indicate to possible areas for product research - a gap for a smooth toothpaste in an automatic dispenser as well as a gap for a coarse toothpaste in an automatic dispenser. There is even a possibility for more coarse toothpastes in the present tubes.

Play around with the **PPM** and see where your product is in the market, and what possible gaps exist in the present market.

Incidentally, most pieces of military equipment have been identified with the use of the **PPM.**

Annexure B
The Product Lifecycle

Every product, even including a human being, the earth, etc. have a specific product lifecycle. The stages in a product's lifecycle are the following:

Research (Planning)
Birth.
Question mark.
Star.
Cash cow.
Dog.

A visual view of the product lifecycle appears in the graphic below:

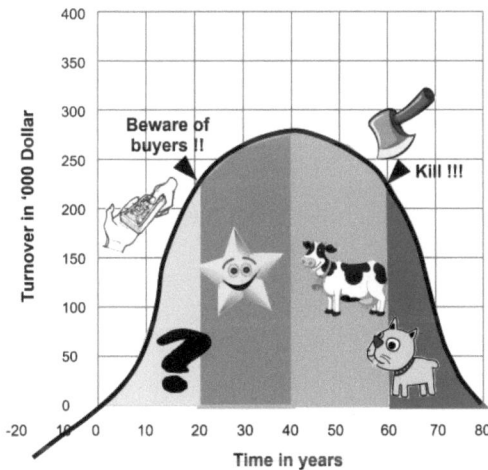

Brief information on each step of the **Product Lifecycle** is as follows:

Research (Planning)

Market research to determine the need of the market and the type of product.
Product development.
Financial planning and price scenarios.
Pilot studies.
Production planning.

Planning (research and development) costs money and can take a long time. Some motor vehicles are developed anything from 40 years before final production!)

Birth

The launch of the product with a bang on a certain date and time.

Question mark

The product has been launched but there is uncertainty about its success.
Marketing costs are extremely high.
Income from the product is still relatively low.
Competitors attack the product in various ways to protect their own products.
The product is a question mark - is it going to survive its early days?

Star

The product has proven itself in the market place and a healthy demand develops for it - it is a Star.
It is eroding the market share of competitors.
Marketing costs are still extremely high.
There is some welcome profit.
The product shows a healthy potential.
Competitors or established entrepreneurs may try to buy the product to protect their own products   or to ride on its success of the new kid on the block (even if they attacked it in its previous stage)

Cash cow

The product is well established and probably the market leader and number one in its class.
The product delivers a healthy income stream and profit. Marketing is maintained.

Income is substantially more than marketing costs.

The product is the Cash cow - it funds the business and other up-and-coming products.
With shrewd marketing, repositioning and cosmetic changes the product's Cash cow stadium can be extended substantially.

Dog

The product nears the end of its productive life.
Other or newer / more modern products are starting to replace it in the market.
No amount of marketing can save a dying product.
Efforts to increase the lifespan of a dog is non-productive.
A dog eats the business's cash.
A dog must be killed instantly and mercifully.

The different stages of a product's life cycle can be of differing duration.

A business should have more than one product on different stages of their lifecycles so that Stars can replace Dogs as they mature and move out of the customer need area.

By managing a product effectively over its lifecycle, more income is realized over a longer period from that product. The aim with marketing is, therefore, to a large extent to launch the product from its present position of its lifecycle to an entirely new orbit with a longer lifecycle and lifespan (see graphic below) thus realizing more income, and higher income, over a longer period.

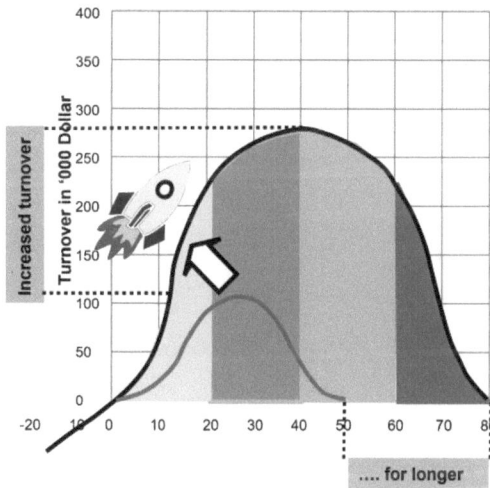

Annexure C
The Marketing Communication Plan

Guidelines are supplied in this document on achieving the 25 goals of the Marketing Communication Plan in the business.

It is by no means a complete list and serves as a general guideline. Each business needs to adapt this communication plan to its own requirements or product / industry needs.

1.   Owner involvement

Purpose: Owners must be actively involved in the business and its management, virtually daily.

What you could do:

1.   Consultations with owner to determine desirable level of owner involvement.

2.   Written undertaking and commitment by owner.

3.   Agreed upon involvement of owner (comprehensive written document), for example:

Personally at office on daily basis.
Dates for scheduled visits to the office.
Day begin and day end procedures and controls.

Reporting requirements.
Budgets.
Financial matters.

4. Schedule monthly meetings with owner.

5. Owner's commitment to professional marketing communication and sufficient marketing expenditure; the marketing budget.

Where the owner(s) are shareholders, different structures will be put in place for instance monthly meetings, reporting, annual general meeting, etc. to address all important aspects.

2. Appoint or designate a senior person with the responsibility of planning and executing marketing communication

Purpose: A key personnel member is appointed to actively drive marketing communication for the business, and he/she is equipped with the necessary authority and decision making power to perform his/her task. In smaller organizations this may not be a fulltime position.

What you could do:

1. Appoint 'Official responsible for marketing' in writing.

2. Supply background information regarding importance of task, company policy and growth strategy etc., ensure official's motivation and involvement, and assure him of the owner's involvement and support.

3. Draft and display a letter of appointment in a prominent place in the office. Inform personnel of appointment.

4. Inform personnel fully of the forthcoming marketing planning. Discuss the appointed official's role, status and tasks, and what is expected of each personnel member.

3. Involve all personnel in the marketing communication planning and execution

Purpose: All personnel, in whatever position, have an influence on customer relations and service, and have knowledge and skills that may be beneficial. Involvement also ensures motivated personnel.

What you could do:

1.   Inform personnel of company's marketing structure and strategy and ensure each personnel member's acceptance and commitment.

2.   Involve personnel in meetings and decision making.

3.   Establish internal communication opportunities.

4.   Hold regular marketing meetings.

4.   All personnel is orientated and trained in marketing communication

Purpose: Present marketing communication orientation and training to key and other personnel according to the needs of their positions and involve all personnel members in the compilation of the marketing plan.

What you could do:

1.   Implement a register for training qualifications and log all successful training of personnel.

2.   Determine need for orientation and training amongst personnel.

3.   Schedule and implement training.

4.   Display all current certificates for training in a prominent place in the office.

5.   Train personnel internally properly to understand the concepts of marketing communication, professionalism, service, client communication and terms such as ethics and etiquette. Provide what is expected of each personnel member in writing and display prominently in the office.

6.   Implement a consultative process whereby all personnel members are involved in the gathering of information and the compilation of the marketing plan.

7.   Retrain personnel annually if required.

8.   Identify personnel members for any form of advanced training and implement that training.

5.   Introduce personnel motivational systems and programs

Purpose: Motivate personnel by a combination of remuneration and acknowledgement systems.

What you could do:

1.   Introduce a remuneration system based on payment for performance.

2.   Develop incentives for personnel such as 'Marketer of the Term', 'Most Friendly Personnel Member' and 'Client Service Champion for the Month.'

3.   Implement value adding staff benefits - medical insurance, pension fund, leave.

4.   Develop career opportunities.

5.   Involve personnel in participating management.

6.   The market is analyzed to determine its needs and potential

Purpose: Analyze the market and determine its potential size and needs for the business's products precisely.

What you could do:

1.   Obtain demographical data for the market.

2.   Survey consumer needs.

3.   Determine the market potential.

4.   Research trends.

7.   The exact target market or operational area of the business is determined

Purpose: Determine the target market precisely, in other words who are the consumers that the business want to serve, and in which geographical area will services be provided.

What you could do:

1.   Obtain a largescale map of the town, suburb or area.

2.   Plot existing customers' places of residence, work, worship, sport and other social activities on the map. Plot their main transport routes and modes of transport between these places on the map.

3.   Plot larger employers, and places where numbers of potential clients may be, on the map.

4.   Draw a block or circle around the areas where the most dots and activity on the map occur. This should be the business' target market or operational area.

5.   Take a policy decision to only operate within this demarcated area and inform personnel accordingly.

6.   Determine any niche markets within the target area whose needs must be addressed differently or for which a separate marketing plan can be implemented. (mine workers, shift workers, people with irregular office hours, certain city streets, certain larger employers, etc.)

8.   Develop and refine the product and product offering according to the market needs

Purpose: Develop the product to optimally comply with the exact needs of the target market.

What you could do:

1.   Determine the core product benefits and focus on it. Do not waste time on secondary products not related to or compatible with the core product.

2.   Develop the marketing promise for customers.

3.   Establish a competitive advantage for the product.

4.   An important product attribute is its accessibility. Suitable office hours are a prerequisite to facilitate this. At larger employers, or for pensioners and shift workers it should be considered to take the product to the market, rather than expect the market to come to the product or the business.

9. Determine the business vision or long term goal

Purpose: A quantifiable and reachable long term goal must be determined for the business.

What you could do:

1. Formulate precise targets regarding:

Market share (to be the largest seller of .... in the area within three years) Look at turnover, number of clients, growth etc. Quantify rather than generalize.

2. Inform each personnel member of this vision and ensure his/her involvement and commitment to participate in reaching these goals.

10. Mission

Purpose: Determine the business' mission or strategy to reach its long term goal or vision.

What you could do:

1. It is the mission of .... to reach its growth target of X% per annum by concentrating on the following critical performance areas:

Professionalism and ethical conduct.
Owner involvement.
Financial management.
Management and control.
Management reports.
Marketing communication.
Training.
Electronic communication.
Growth.

This will be achieved by all personnel becoming involved in training and the marketing communications process.

2. The owner of the business and each personnel member commit themselves and sign a **Document of Intent** to achieve the aims and targets, which is prominently displayed on the business premises.

**11.	Draw the breakeven graph for the business and determine growth targets**

Purpose: The growth targets that must be reached, are broken down into smaller, achievable figures/actions

What you could do:

1.	Draw the breakeven graph using actual monthly figures for the office.

2.	Specific overall targets are set against a time frame, and broken down per department, section, employee and completion dates.

3.	Break this target number down into:

Per month.
Per week.
Per day.

4.	Decide on the targets after consultation with personnel.

**12.	Incorporate marketing communication as a core function in all personnel's duty sheets**

Purpose: Each employee is in the first instance a marketer for the business and his/her duty sheet should reflect this.

What you could do:

1.	Rewrite duty sheets to start with:

The employee is in the first instance a marketer and marketing communicator for the business, and it is expected of him/her to continuously, positively and effectively contribute to the business' marketing by:
Contributing to the compilation of the marketing plan.
Professional conduct.
Excellent client service.
Involvement with marketing, communication, actions and campaigns.

(Then followed by the other duties of the position)

13. Work according to and provide funding for marketing communication in a marketing budget

Purpose: A realistic amount must be made available monthly and utilized effectively for marketing. It is not good enough to see what can be saved elsewhere for marketing.

What you could do:

1. Determine an amount that can under the current circumstances be realistically allocated to marketing.

2. Determine which additional amount is going to be realized out of the increased turnover, can be allocated to marketing (this should be more than the first amount as all fixed costs of the business have already been accounted for)

3. Increase the amount monthly or from time to time as turnover increases.

4. Decide in advance and in principle never to decrease the available amount for marketing. There are many other ways to save rather than to cut back on an investment in marketing.

14. Maintain the corporate identity immaculately

Purpose: The corporate identity (trade names / colors / logo's / slogans / directives of corporate manual) is the cornerstone of a business' marketing communication. It ensures visibility and a professional image, which is the largest single contributing factor to success.

What you could do:

1. Create a professional corporate image, if need be by making use of professionals in these fields.

2. Create a corporate manual with directives on the use of the logo, slogans etc in advertising, on stationary etc.

3. Furbish the inside and the outside of the business according to the directives of the corporate manual.

4. The business must be visible from at least 100 meters and three directions.

5.   Increase the visibility by signs on the sidewalk, advertisements on dustbins, flags, signs etc.

6.   Always keep the interior and the exterior of the office properly maintained. Replace faded, rusted and torn material regularly.

7.   Obtain the consent of the personnel to wear corporate clothing.

15.   Dominate continuously in your target area

Purpose: Dominate continuously in the target area with outdoor advertising, and advertising and promotions to obtain maximum exposure and to counter competitors

What you could do:

1.   Erect outdoor advertising at *'hot spots'* and prominent places within the target area, for example at stations, taxi ranks, large shopping complexes, sports fields etc.

This includes advertising boards, posters, advertisements on dustbins, taxi's etc.

A potential customer on his way between his home and place of work must not

travel for longer than 10 minutes without being exposed to an advertisement of your business or product.

2.   Distribute adequate numbers of promotional material and items effectively in the target area to encourage potential customers to visit the office. Use pamphlets, marketing cards, brochures, gifts and handouts.

Distribute in front of business, on street, at factory gates, at exhibitions, at bus and taxi ranks and stations etc.

3.   Obtain the addresses and readership or listener numbers of local media such as newspapers and radio stations, as well as the relevant advertising rates.

4.   Determine through a sample survey which newspapers customers read and to which radio stations they listen.

5.   Advertise selectively in the identified media.   Consider competitions, sponsorships and promotions to direct customers to the business premises.

16. Establish your affiliation program for champions and infiltrate areas where large numbers of consumers congregate

Purpose: Satisfied clients in key positions at larger employers can become champions and can contribute immensely to recruiting new customers in exchange for specific benefits.

What you could do:

1.	Identify existing suitable customers at employers, clubs or associations such as team leaders, foremen etc.

2.	Involve them as ***champions*** to operate as your freelance agents.

3.	Develop incentives at different levels for champions.

17. Maintain the service concept and delight the customers

Purpose: Customers base their patronage of a business largely on the quality of service and support provided by the business, and not necessarily on price.

What you could do:

1.	Compile a service manual for the business.

2.	Inform and involve all personnel members of the service expectations.

3.	Take note of consumer rights, acknowledge them and instill them.

4.	Ensure that the business' service is perceived by the customer as value for money. Customers must feel that they are welcome, important, treated well and rewarded for their support. Use gifts, cold drinks and refreshments on certain times during the month, etc.

5.	Evaluate the business' service regularly amongst customers.

18. Implement a sound public relations program

Purpose: Good public relations is required to form a healthy public image for the business in the broader community and creates the climate for

healthy business.   A comprehensive and purposeful public relations program must be in place.

What you could do:

1.   Identify relevant media in the target area (see above)

2.   Identify opinion formers of importance/ organizations of importance in the target area, for instance mayor, chamber of commerce, etc.

3.   Meet and become the friend of the decision makers in the media.

4.   Identify or create newsworthy material to enhance the business' public image such as donations to mayoral charity funds, sponsorships, donations to the needy, release of annual figures, promotions, etc.

5.   Communicate with opinion makers at meetings, with specific publications etc.

6.   Have a senior company spokesperson to prepare press releases and speak to the media

7.   Never say 'no comment' to a journalist. You are just inviting negative press.

19.   Accept and practice social responsibility

Purpose: From a moral point of view it is essential for organizations that obtain their income from a certain sector, to reinvest some of its profit in

that sector, and for that matter their customer base. These activities are of the utmost importance and must also be utilized to obtain maximum positive exposure for the business.

What you could do:

1.   Identify projects with large publicity value to selectively underscore the marketing effort. Consider donations to disaster funds, transport for pensioners, adult education, assistance for the needy, contributions to wildlife and the environment etc.

The sponsorship must for publicity purposes be related to your business activities.

2.   Ensure adequate media coverage for the business.

3.   Manage sponsorships contractually on an ongoing basis.

20. Study, monitor and counter competitors

Purpose: The business must be the market leader in all respects. Competitors should only be following the leader in their actions. The business' activities must be directed at drawing customers away from competitors.

What you could do:

1.   Compile a complete list of all competitors within the target area of the business.

2.   Open a file for each competitor.

3.   Gather information on the competitors and place it. on their files: Their numbers of staff members and customers, their marketing activities, their products, their strong and weak points, copies of their advertising material, etc.

4.   Identify and institute actions to counter the competitor's marketing actions, or, as a prevention, implement your own marketing activities.

21.   Co-ordinate marketing

Purpose: When drafting the business' marketing communication plan, co-ordinate with the different departments and all personnel.

What you could do:

1.   Co-ordinate marketing communication with all relevant personnel and stakeholders.

2.   Hold a weekly Marketing Communication Meeting.

22.   Introduce work schedules

Purpose: Work schedules for all aspects of the marketing communication plan should be compiled. Tasks are added to this list during the weekly marketing meeting and remains on the list until completed. Other tasks can be monitored by using the same document.

What you could do:

1.   Obtain work schedules and adapt for use by the business.

2.   All the business' marketing aids or tools and projects are listed on the work sheet. Target markets or areas to be addressed are listed separately.

3.   Marketing for the forthcoming period is usually planned during the weekly marketing meeting and work sheets compiled. The previous week's activities are also evaluated.

4.   Also see 24 below.

23.   Introduce management by objectives

Purpose: Productivity is increased and personnel motivated when clear targets are set.

What you could do:

1.   Set clear targets and dates regarding sales, turnover, income etc.

2.   Devise a system of remuneration for achievement.

3.   Inform all personnel of targets and benefits.

4.   Monitor achievements.

24.   Measure results and trends

Purpose: Each facet of the marketing communication plan must be evaluated to determine its success or failure.

What you could do:

1.   During the weekly marketing meeting, evaluate all current and completed activities.

2. Plan the activities for two to three weeks ahead. A work sheet is used for each week.

3.   Include all new tasks or projects in the work sheet, including target dates, responsible person and expected costs.

4.   Determine precisely which activities resulted in the recruitment of new customers or increased sales.

5.   Determine the cost-effectiveness of these activities, in other words divide the expenditure by the total number of customers or sales.

6.   Personnel members are continuously evaluated in a similar manner.

7.   Keep expenditure under control and within the marketing budget. Annotate each expense as a percentage of the monthly marketing budget.

8.   Do regular research surveys of the different target areas.

9.   Stop ineffective marketing activities

25.   Adapt

Purpose: Adapt to changing conditions or circumstances or your business will die.

What you could do:

1.   Continue with successful marketing communication and stop unsuccessful marketing communication.

2.   Retrain unproductive personnel and evaluate them again. If no improvement, replace with better equipped personnel.

3.   Follow the guidelines obtained from continuous research for adapting and positioning your business for the future.

4.   Continuously adapt the marketing projects to ensure optimal efficiency.

oooooOOOooooo

Annexure D
The Break Even Graph

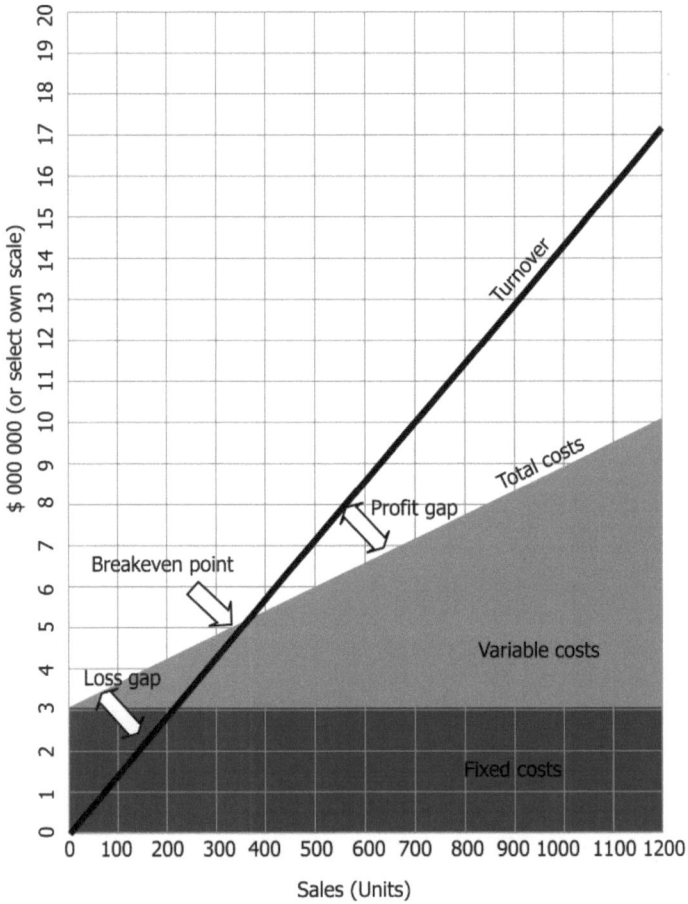

Annexure E
Some Important Hints

Beware of a price war

There are many ways to market and increase sales before a drastic step such as price reduction is contemplated.

When prices are cut, you are either following competitors, or inviting competitors to follow you, creating a "price war". Everyone bleeds, and it only depends on who can bleed the most before he dies. Irreparable harm is done to both businesses.

Do not fall into the discount trap!

A 50% mark up on an item of $100 at cost, increases the selling price for the consumer to $150. A 50% discount on the $150 Dollar selling price, however, does not revert the price back to $100. It brings the price down to a low $75 Dollar, $25 Dollar below cost and a loss. Beware of this trap and don't give price discounts to your best friends and find out later that the product was, in fact, sold well below cost price and at a loss!

A mark-up of 150% allows for a discount of 60%
A mark-up of 100% allows for a discount of 50%
A mark-up of 75% allows for a discount of 43%
A mark-up of 50% allows for a discount of 33%
A mark-up of 40% allows for a discount of 28%

The Company logo

The company logo is the crown jewel in the company's marketing effort. It is the emblem by which the company is identified, and it must attract immediate attention and be memorable. It must talk to the customer.

The image must preferably be related to your company's activities, and the company name, or initials, must appear in or together with the logo.

The logo consists of shapes, letters/words and colors:

Shapes:

Different shapes convey different messages to customers, as follows:

Circles and ovals - friendliness.
Triangles - leadership and authority.
Squares and rectangles - security, efficiency and trustworthiness.
Curved lines - relaxation, playfulness.
Spikes or angles - aggression.
Horizontal lines - stability
Vertical lines - success, prosperity

The shape can include elements or cues to inform customers of your type of business, such as drawings or outlines of a fish for a fish hatchery, a hat for a tailor, etc.

Fonts

There are basically four types of fonts, namely Serifs, Sans Serifs, Script or Handwritten. A serif is a stroke or addition to a letter that either provides a foot for the letters to stand on, or additional strokes added to the letters of the font. Serif fonts are more elaborate, sometimes difficult to read and does not reduce well in size.

San Serif simply means 'without serifs', resulting in a range of clean fonts.

San Serif fonts convey messages of 'formal', 'classical' and 'traditional' to the customer. Serif fonts convey messages of 'modern' 'efficient' and 'casual'

Script fonts are regarded as fancy, and handwritten fonts as casual or friendly.

Colors

Traditionally colors are broadly associated with certain emotions or activities:

Yellow - confidence, sunshine and warmth, a children's favorite.
Orange - excitement, adventure, optimism, vitality
Brown - comforting, nature conservation, soil and land.
Green - health, tranquility, life, living and growth, the color of money
Red - power, movement, excitement, urgency, alertness and passion.
Purple - royalty, wisdom, respect, problem-solving, death, funerals
Blue - credibility, peace, tranquility, reliability, productivity, the preferred color of men.
Gold - power and royalty
White - cleanliness, purity, safety.
Black - authority, stability, confidence and strength.
Gray - practicality, solidarity – but beware, can bring about depression.

Whatever logo you create for your company image, make sure that:

It is unique and easily distinguishable
It is adaptable to large and small sizes
That a suitable black and white version can be created
That it can be used on all the company's marketing material such as stationary, vehicle livery, banners, store fronts, brochures, pamphlets annual reports etc.
That it does not offend any language, religious, cultural, sexual or disability group.

Subtle changes can be made to the corporate image over time without the customers even noticing it. If large scale changes to the corporate image are envisaged, then it needs to be accompanied by a specific public relations and marketing campaign over a period of time, first to inform and get the support of the staff, and then secondly to introduce customers to the change and allow them time to become familiar with it.

Slogan

These are, according to research, the top advertising slogans of all tim

1. Adidas - Impossible is nothing
2. Ajax - Stronger than dirt
3. Airbnb - Belong anywhere
4. Alka Seltzer - I can't believe I ate the whole thing
5. Allstate - You're in good hands
6. American Express - Don't leave home without it
7. Apple - Think different
8. Avis - We try harder
9. BMW - The ultimate driving machine
10. Bounty - The quicker picker-upper
11. Burger King - Have it your way
12. Campbell's Soup - Mmm, mmm good!
13. Capital One - What's in your wallet?
14. Chevrolet - The heartbeat of America
15. Clairol - Does she or doesn't she?
16. Coca-Cola - Open happiness
17. De Beers - A diamond is forever
18. Disneyland - The happiest place on earth
19. Dunkin' Donuts - America runs on Dunkin'
20. Energizer - It keeps going... and going... and going
21. Facebook - Move fast and break things
22. Fed-Ex - When it absolutely, positively has to be there overnight
23. Frosted Flakes - They're grrrrrrreat!
24. Gatorade - Is it in you?
25. Geico - So easy a caveman can do it

26. General Electric - We bring good things to life

27. Google - Don't be evil

28. John Deere - Nothing runs like a deer

29. Kay Jewelers - Every kiss begins with Kay

30. Kentucky Fried Chicken - Finger lickin' good

31. Lexus - The relentless pursuit of perfection

32. L'Oreal - Because you're worth it

33. Lay's Potato Chips - Betcha can't eat just one

34. M&Ms - Melts in your mouth, not in your hands

35. Maxwell House - Good to the last drop

36. McDonald's - I'm lovin' it

37. Morton Salt - When it rains, it pours

38. Nike - Just do it

39. Pepsi - The choice of a new generation

40. Rice Krispies - Snap! Crackle! Pop!

41. Skittles - Taste the rainbow

42. Sprite - Obey your thirst

43. Timex - Takes a licking and keeps on ticking

44. Trix Cereal - Trix are for kids

45. United Airlines - Fly the friendly skies

46. UPS - What can brown do for you?

47. Verizon Mobile - Can you hear me now?

48. Volkswagen - Think small

49. Wendy's - Where's the beef?

50. Wheaties - The breakfast of champions

A slogan or tagline is a short reminder to the customer of your product and service promise.

If you require a slogan for your company, follow these guidelines:

Keep it short and simple
Use an understandable language, not Latin or Greek.
Use simple, everyday words
Do not try to be funny
Beware of puns and wordplay